Elizabeth Ripley

DURER

DURER

A Biography by **ELIZABETH RIPLEY**

With Paintings, Etchings and Drawings by **ALBRECHT DURER**

J. B. LIPPINCOTT COMPANY · Philadelphia · New York

ACKNOWLEDGEMENTS

The author wishes to thank Dr. Einar Hille of Yale University, New Haven, for his assistance in translating correspondence with German photographers and museums, and Dr. Erwin Panofsky, The Institute of Advanced Study, Princeton, for his helpful advice regarding the choice of illustrations in this book.

ILLUSTRATIONS

ONE DAY in 1475 a goldsmith named Albrecht Dürer opened a workshop in his new tall, gabled house in the center of Nuremberg in Germany. The silent goldsmith set to work immediately carving elaborate designs on golden goblets and silver shields, while his pretty young wife bustled from room to room settling the house for her husband and their three children.

Dürer's youngest child was a handsome, merry boy of three, who was named for his father. Albrecht Dürer loved his little son and hoped that some day the boy would become a famous goldsmith. When young Albrecht was old enough his father sent him to school; and as soon as he learned to read and write, Dürer decided it was time to teach his son the goldsmith's trade.

In his father's workshop Albrecht learned how to carve delicate designs on pieces of hard metal. With a steady hand the boy guided the sharp cutting tool, and Dürer marveled at his son's skill. But Albrecht often wished he could make illustrations for books instead of digging out designs on metal. In the evenings his mother would find him bent over a piece of paper sketching gay pictures of knights in armor and lords and ladies on horseback.

One day when he was thirteen years old, Albrecht sat in front of a mirror and drew a picture of himself. His little face was serious, for he knew that the fine lines of his silver point pencil could not be erased. With a sure hand he drew the thin lines of his long hair and each fold in the wide sleeves of his tunic. His mother was delighted with her son's portrait, but Albrecht thought that the drawing of the hand looked awkward and the folds of the blouse stiff. He knew that he still had much to learn.

Some years later he wrote in the corner of the first portrait he had ever made:

"I drew myself from the mirror in the year 1484, when I was still a child. Albrecht Dürer."

SELF PORTRAIT
    Silver Point Drawing. 1484
    Albertina, Vienna

NEAR the Dürer home lived a boy, one year older than Albrecht, whose name was Willibald Pirckheimer. Willibald and Albrecht often played together and as they grew older they became fast friends. Willibald, son of one of Nuremberg's richest citizens, was fat and domineering, but Dürer admired his quick wit and keen mind and Willibald was attracted by Albrecht's talent, his easy charm and gentle humor.

Willibald loaned his friend books from his father's library. Albrecht loved to study the pictures in Willibald's books and he often copied the illustrations by the famous artist Schongauer. When Willibald saw his friend's drawings he urged him to study art, but Albrecht knew that his father would not want his son to give up the goldsmith's trade.

Albrecht was fifteen when at last he decided to ask his father to let him study art. The goldsmith "was not well pleased," Albrecht wrote years later, "however, he gave in to me."

One winter day in 1486 Albrecht went to study in the studio of Nuremberg's well-known artist Michael Wolgemut. He soon learned to grind and mix paints and how to carve pictures on wood blocks so that they could be printed many times. His teacher was pleased that his new pupil learned so quickly. But Wolgemut's others pupils were jealous of his talent. They were coarse and ill-mannered and often teased the young boy unmercifully. For three years gentle Albrecht silently endured the crude jokes of the apprentices, for he was anxious to learn everything that Wolgemut had to teach him.

When he walked about Nuremberg, Albrecht sketched everything he saw. Sometimes he washed transparent water colors over his precise drawings.

One day he painted a neat little scene of a wire factory by a river. Every detail was clearly drawn. The white timber-trimmed buildings with steep, sloping roofs looked as if they had been cut out of cardboard and placed against a background of rolling hills, green trees and pointed church spires. In the foreground chickens were feeding in the factory courtyard, and an armored knight was fording the river.

WIRE DRAWING MILL
Water Color. 1489
Kupferstichkabinett, Berlin

On warm summer evenings Albrecht used to take long walks into the country. He often paused to note some brightly colored bird in a branch overhead, or study a furry squirrel as it nibbled nervously on an acorn. Sometimes he brought home a piece of turf on which a wild flower was growing and made detailed drawings of the plant before it faded.

On winter evenings Albrecht sat by the fire drawing portraits of his family. He drew pictures of his mother and of his younger brothers and sisters. He painted a portrait of his father dressed in his best fur cap and fur-lined coat. The austere goldsmith held a rosary in his worn hands, to show that he was saying his prayers.

"He was a taciturn and God-fearing man," Albrecht once wrote about his father.

Albrecht was eighteen years old at the time he painted his father's portrait. When the goldsmith saw the finished painting he told his son that his pictures were good enough to sell. So one day in 1490, Albrecht Dürer, the artist, said good-by to his family and set out in search of success.

PORTRAIT OF DURER'S FATHER
1490
Uffizi, Florence

ALBRECHT rode across Germany until he reached the town of Colmar, home of the famous illustrator Schongauer. He longed to meet the great artist whose pictures he had copied, but when he finally arrived in Colmar he was told that Schongauer had died. The artist's brothers welcomed Albrecht warmly, for they had heard about Wolgemut's talented pupil. They introduced him to other artists and to printers who bought some of Dürer's drawings.

Albrecht set to work drawing pictures on wood blocks for illustrations. His clean firm lines stood out boldly when the wood around them was cut away. He strove constantly to improve his drawing. He sketched everything he saw—dogs and cats, his own hands or the folds in a piece of drapery. Often he became depressed, fearing he would never achieve perfection in his work.

One day he drew a picture of himself. Holding his hand to his cheek he studied his face intently. He was only twenty years old, but he looked years older. His troubled eyes seemed to be searching for something he could not find.

Dürer stayed in Colmar for two years. Then one day he set off for Switzerland, because his friends had told him about a famous company of bookmakers in the city of Basle. The Swiss publishers received Dürer cordially and asked him to illustrate some of their books.

Dürer did not stay long in Basle, because he wanted to visit other cities in Switzerland and Germany. For two years he traveled from town to town, selling his drawings and making friends with artists and printers. Then one day he received word that his father wanted him to return to Nuremberg so that he could meet the girl whom the goldsmith had chosen to be young Albrecht Dürer's wife.

SELF PORTRAIT
    Pen Drawing. 1492
    Erlangen University Library

AGNES FREY was the daughter of wealthy Hans Frey, owner of a metal factory in Nuremberg. Hans often visited Dürer's workshop and had known young Albrecht when the boy was working for his father. In Dürer's day parents often arranged their children's marriages, so when Albrecht's works became known in Germany, Hans Frey decided that the talented artist would make a good husband for his daughter. The goldsmith was delighted to accept Agnes Frey for a daughter-in-law.

But when Albrecht returned to Nuremberg, Agnes greeted her future husband coldly. Although she was attracted by his good looks and gentle manner, she was not interested in marrying a man chosen by her father. Albrecht, charmed by this distant but beautiful girl with red-gold hair, waited patiently for her answer. At last Agnes sullenly gave in to her father's wishes, and one summer day in 1495 Agnes and Albrecht were married. Albrecht brought his bride to live in his father's home.

Agnes was not interested in Albrecht's work, nor did she care for his noisy friend Willibald who talked about books, philosophy and art. So Dürer spent many hours at the Pirckheimer home, where he met distinguished scholars and writers from many countries. Willibald urged his friend to take a trip to Italy, so that he could see the works of the great Italian artists. Agnes did not seem to care that her husband wanted to leave Nuremberg only a few months after their marriage; so one fall day Albrecht said good-by to his wife and set off across the mountains toward Venice.

Dürer loved the glittering warmth of Venice. He sketched the exotic costumes he saw on the streets and made detailed drawings of fashionably dressed Venetian ladies. He picked up strange shellfish on the seashore and made a drawing of a giant crab and another of a lobster.

Through the mild winter months Dürer stayed in Venice, sketching what he saw and copying the pictures of Italian artists. When spring came, he wrote Agnes that he was returning to Nuremberg.

VENETIAN LADY
  Pen Drawing. 1495
  Albertina, Vienna

THE WARM spring sun was melting the snow when Dürer rode over the mountains towards Nuremberg. As his horse climbed slowly up a narrow road, Albrecht looked down on brilliant green valleys and on lakes and winding rivers which reflected the radiant blue sky overhead. From time to time he gave his horse a rest, while he made a sketch of a turn in the steep road or of a row of trees beside a quiet lake.

Albrecht traveled slowly. Sometimes he stayed for several days in a town where he wished to paint a water color. Everything he saw was bathed in the fresh brilliance of spring, and he wanted to show this luminous atmosphere in his pictures. Early one morning he painted a vine-covered castle high on a mountain. Its pointed turrets were silhouetted against a clear blue sky. He painted the towers and roofs of the town of Trent, nestled at the foot of snow-covered mountains.

One day he sat on the banks of the River Inn and painted the city of Innsbruck. With care he drew each turret and spire of the walled town, and then with a brush he washed on the shimmering reflection in the water below and the soft clouds in the blue sky above.

INNSBRUCK SEEN FROM THE NORTH
   Water Color. 1494
      Albertina, Vienna

DURER rode into Nuremberg one spring day in 1495, carrying a case filled with clean crisp water colors which told the story of his trip across the mountains. He filed his sketches carefully, for he knew that he would use these landscapes as backgrounds in his illustrations.

He set to work making wood block drawings, and the castles, streams and mountains which he had painted appeared in many of his pictures.

When he had time Dürer painted water colors of scenes around Nuremberg. The skies seemed cool and grey compared with the bright Italian skies but everywhere Dürer looked he saw rich transparent color. He painted a quiet pond at sunset time. The clear water mirrored the rosy glow of the setting sun. On a small green island stood a tiny house, its pointed roof reflected in the pink water.

Early one morning Albrecht painted a lake in the woods. As the bright rays of the rising sun broke through purple clouds, the colors of the water changed constantly. With broad strokes he washed on the deep blues, bright oranges and rich purples of the sky and water; and with a finely pointed brush he painted each delicate blade of grass in the foreground and the trunks of the tall pine trees growing beside the lake. But before Dürer could block in the dark green branches against a flaming sky, the sunrise glow had disappeared.

Although Dürer never finished the picture of the pond in the woods, this luminous sketch of water, trees and sky is one of the most romantic landscapes he ever painted.

POND IN WOODS
Water Color. 1495
British Museum, London

THE PALE RAYS of the autumn sun filtered through the leaded windowpanes of the room where Dürer sat working. With a pointed chisel he was drawing a picture on a piece of metal. His steady hand guided the sharp tool which dug out clean grooves in the copper-plate. He worked without stopping, for he was anxious to finish this plate which would be used to print his drawing many times. Dürer knew that he would be able to sell the printed drawings, and hoped in this way to make enough money to buy a home for himself and Agnes.

When the plate was finished Dürer took it to a printer. The printer rubbed ink into the grooves of the polished metal. Then he carefully placed a sheet of dampened paper on top of the inked plate and rolled it through his press. When he lifted the sheet from the plate, Dürer could see that every fine line of his drawing had been printed on the paper. This printed drawing was called an engraving.

All through the cold winter months Dürer worked on his engravings. One showed a soldier talking to a lady on horse-back and another a peasant scolding his disagreeble wife. He engraved a lovely picture of the Virgin with the baby Jesus against a background of river, hills, and castles. Albrecht's mother often sat in a booth at the Nuremberg market and sold her son's prints to travelers from many countries. Soon the engravings of Albrecht Dürer were well known in Europe.

One of Dürer's finest engravings told the Bible story of the Prodigal Son. This reckless young man, having spent all the money his father had given him, had not dared to return home. When he begged for work at the home of a stranger, he was sent out into the fields to feed the pigs. The engraving showed a young man with long wavy hair, who looked like Dürer, kneeling beside a crude trough where pigs were feeding. The hungry youth, leaning on his staff, implored God to forgive him for his sins. In the background was a group of untidy farm buildings, which looked like the miserable homes of the poor peasants of Nuremberg.

PRODIGAL SON
  Engraving. 1496
  Courtesy of the Metropolitan Museum of Art, New York

In the spring of 1496, Frederick, Duke of Saxony, visited the city of Nuremberg. This kindly ruler, who was called Frederick the Wise, had admired Albrecht Dürer's engravings and was anxious to have his portrait painted by the talented young artist.

Dürer's picture showed the bearded duke wearing a black tunic trimmed with gold and a black cap. His expression was austere, but Frederick was so pleased with the portrait that he commissioned Dürer to paint two pictures for a church in Saxony. So eager was Albrecht to fill Frederick's order promptly, that he hired an assistant to help him finish one of the paintings. Soon two large altarpieces were ready for the church.

Dürer was so well paid for his work that he was able to rent a big workshop in the center of Nuremberg. He hired assistants and bought a press, so that he could print his own engravings. One day he visited Willibald's tailor and ordered an expensive suit of clothes.

Albrecht painted a picture of himself wearing his new white tunic trimmed with black, a tan cloak and a black and white striped cap. His chestnut colored hair fell in tight waves over his shoulders and his beard and moustache were neatly trimmed. Beyond an open window in the background was a view of river, sky and snow-capped mountains, which looked like the lanscapes Dürer had seen in Italy. Albrecht's expression was serious but confident, for this handsome, well-dressed young man knew that he was now a successful artist. In a space just below the window Dürer wrote in neat clear letters:

"This I painted after my image. I was six-and-twenty years old. Albrecht Dürer."

SELF PORTRAIT
1498
Prado, Madrid

THE PEASANTS of Nuremberg were desperately poor in the year 1498. Their crops failed and many farmers died of hunger. All over Germany peasants rose up against the rich landowners. Then a terrible plague swept through the country, striking down rich and poor alike. Some people thought that famine, war and plague were signs from God to warn man of the approaching Day of Judgment. Many people believed that when the century ended the world would be destroyed.

As the year 1500 drew near, men and women looked for comfort in the Bible. They found an answer to their troubled thoughts in the hopeful words of Saint John the Divine, who wrote the strange and beautiful book called *The Apocalypse* or *Revelation*. Saint John told of how God revealed to him terrible visions of the end of the world; but when the fearful day of judgment was over, God showed him a new world where there was no misery and sorrow. Dürer longed to illustrate Saint John's visions. He imagined a big picture book which would tell the story of *The Apocalypse*.

In two years Dürer designed fifteen brilliant woodcuts which illustrated Saint John's prophetic visions. He pictured four hideous galloping horsemen. The first was War, carrying a bow and arrow; the second Sickness, wielding a mighty sword; the third, swinging a pair of scales, represented Hunger; and in front rode the gruesome figure of Death. Men, women and even kings were trampled under the horses' hooves as the four riders plunged on. Then Dürer pictured a vision of fire, blood and locusts raining down upon the earth and of angels armed with swords, mowing down bishops, knights and kings. Finally Dürer illustrated a vision of a furious battle between Saint Michael and a dragon which represented the devil.

Dürer's last picture showed Saint John looking upon a new and peaceful world. In the foreground an angel pushed the vanquished dragon into a pit, while in the background another angel pointed out to the saint a new and shining city in the quiet valley below.

THE FOUR HORSEMEN OF THE APOCALYPSE
Woodcut. 1498
Courtesy of the Metropolitan Museum of Art, New York

Princes and scholars, merchants and bankers bought copies of Dürer's *Apocalypse*. On the back of each picture was printed the Bible text which described St. John's visions. In some of the books the text was printed in German and in others it was in Latin. So clearly did Dürer's pictures illustrate every detail of the Bible text that even the people who could not read were able to understand St. John's strange visions.

Other artists marveled at the brilliance of Dürer's prints and wondered how, without the help of color, he was able to show clouds and fire and flashing lightning.

"These things he places before the eye in the most pertinent lines," wrote the scholar Erasmus, "so that if you should spread on pigments, you would injure the work."

Dürer painted only a few pictures while he was working on his woodcuts; but two years after the *Apocalypse* was finished he painted a portrait of himself. On a smooth panel of wood he drew a beautifully proportioned head. The oval face was framed by a short beard and long wavy hair, but it did not look like the face of the stylish gentleman Dürer had painted two years before. The deep searching eyes were rounder, the nose straighter. Dürer did not picture himself as he was; instead he made a portrait of himself as he would like to appear.

When his drawing of the ideal man was finished he colored it with layer upon layer of thin, transparent paint. The coat was tan, the background a deep brown. Then with a fine brush he painted each strand of his chestnut curls and the soft shiny bristles of his brown fur collar.

When the last colored glaze had dried, Dürer lettered neatly in the corner of his picture, "I, Albrecht Dürer of Nuremberg, painted my own portrait here in the proper colors at the age of twenty-eight."

SELF PORTRAIT
1500
Alte Pinakothek, Munich

THE WORLD did not come to an end in the year 1500, and the people who had dreaded the beginning of a new century became less anxious. Dürer no longer pictured terrifying visions of the Day of Judgment. Instead he designed a book of woodcuts illustrating the life of the Virgin. They were serene pictures filled with details of family life. One showed the Virgin dressed in the clothes of a Nuremberg housewife, sitting in the courtyard of a carpenter's shop. She was spinning busily as she rocked the baby Jesus' cradle with her foot. Behind her was her husband Joseph who was splintering wood at his workbench. Another picture showed the Holy Family on its way to Egypt. The Virgin, holding her child in her arms, rode on a donkey which Joseph was leading. A patient ox plodded beside them.

Dürer loved to fill his pictures with plants and animals and bits of landscapes. In a huge engraving he illustrated the legend of Saint Eustace and the stag. The story told of how one day a Roman soldier was hunting in a forest when suddenly a stag appeared before him. Between the deer's antlers was a cross on which was nailed the body of Christ. The stag spoke to the hunter, urging him to believe in Christ. The soldier, deeply moved by the miracle, promised to become a Christian.

Dürer's big engraving of Saint Eustace showed a beautiful landscape filled with different kinds of animals. Five hunting dogs and the hunter's horse filled the foreground. Two swans were swimming in a pool behind the hunter and a flock of birds circled around the castle in the background.

SAINT EUSTACE
Engraving. About 1501
Courtesy of the Metropolitan Museum of Art, New York

OVER AND OVER animals appeared in Dürer's woodcuts and engravings. He filled sketchbooks with drawings of the animals he saw around him. He drew a sleek greyhound, a stately elk and a parrot sitting on a perch. For a long time he studied a hare as it sat quietly, its long ears pointing upward and its front feet placed neatly together. Later he painted a water color of this hare. With a fine brush he drew every soft hair of its furry coat and each long quivering whisker. Every detail of the animal was precisely painted, yet the sensitive creature seemed wonderfully alive.

HARE
    Water Color. 1502
    Albertina, Vienna

Early one morning Agnes knocked loudly on Albrecht's door. His father was very ill, she told her husband, and his mother wanted Albrecht to come to his room immediately. Dürer hurried downstairs to his father's room. A few days later, Albrecht Dürer the goldsmith died.

"He was a clever master of his craft," Albrecht wrote about his father, "having nothing for his support save what he earned with his hand."

So as soon as Albrecht had sold his father's shop, he set to work making more engravings, so that he could support his mother and her younger children.

Then suddenly Albrecht fell ill. For weeks his mother watched anxiously at her son's bedside. At last his fever left him, but he felt too weak to work on his engravings. On sunny spring days he sat in the little garden behind his house and marveled at the beauty of the plants and animals he saw around him. The differences in animals fascinated him. He never tired of watching how they were made and how they moved.

Albrecht drew a charming picture of the Virgin Mary and her baby in a garden, surrounded by all sorts of little animals. A parrot was perched on a stick beside the Virgin, a small fox, tied to a stake, was examining a snail. A beetle tickled the nose of a shaggy dog which lay at the Virgin's feet and an owl stared wide-eyed from a hollow stump. In the background Joseph was talking to a stork and a ram was charging a sheep dog on the hill in the distance. On top of the hill shepherds received the news of Christ's birth from an angel which descended from the sky.

Over this pen drawing Dürer washed delicate water-color tints, which were so transparent that every detail of this charming picture could be clearly seen.

MADONNA WITH A MULTITUDE OF ANIMALS
   Drawing. About 1503
   Albertina, Vienna

WHEN DURER felt strong enough to walk to his studio he began once more to work on his engravings.

The bulky figure of Pirckheimer often darkened the doorway of Dürer's workshop, for Willibald loved to suggest subjects for his friend's engravings and talk to him about some essay he wanted Albrecht to illustrate. Sometimes he commissioned Dürer to decorate the margins of his books and he asked his friend to design a bookplate for his library. Dürer was never too busy to argue with his learned friend about art, philosophy and books.

"What you say cannot be painted!" Pirckheimer once roared.

"No," replied Albrecht quietly, "what you state cannot be put into words or even figured in the mind."

One day Willibald asked Albrecht to draw his portrait in profile, so that later it could be engraved on a medal. Dürer, whose eyes were tired after drawing the fine lines of an engraving, picked up a sheet of paper and a blunt stick of charcoal. In broad sweeping strokes he drew the outline of his friend's massive head. Then with his finger he lightly smeared the lines under the double chin, the hollows of the ear and the curve of the nostril. This subtle shading gave form to the vigorous profile.

Dürer drew his friend exactly as he saw him. The thickset face was far from handsome, but it was the face of a forceful and keenly intelligent man.

WILLIBALD PIRCKHEIMER
Charcoal Drawing. 1503
Kupferstichkabinett, Berlin

A PICTURE IN SHADES of brown stood on an easel in Dürer's workshop. It showed the Three Kings worshipping the Christ Child. For weeks Dürer had been working on the painting which Frederick the Wise had ordered for a church in Saxony.

As if he were working on an engraving, Dürer drew every detail with care. The plants growing on the stone archways in the background, the grasshopper, the butterflies and a large beetle in the foreground were clearly shown. Then one day, Dürer started to color the picture with coats of brilliant paint. The Virgin's dress became an azure blue, the coat of the king who tenderly embraced the Christ Child was a rich red, and the cloak of the Moorish king a dark green. A young king, who looked like Dürer, stood in the center of the picture wearing a gold brocaded tunic with bright green sleeves. Frederick the Wise was delighted with the picture and paid Dürer generously.

More and more commissions poured into Dürer's workshop. A rich German merchant wrote him about an altarpiece which he wanted Albrecht to paint for the German church in Venice. Dürer longed to see the glittering city which he had visited when he was a student, eleven years before.

Willibald promised to watch out for Albrecht's family while his friend was in Italy. He offered to lend Dürer money for the trip, and commissioned him to bring back rugs, rare books and antique coins for his collection. So one spring day in 1505, Albrecht set off for Venice.

ADORATION OF THE MAGI
1504
Uffizi, Florence

"OH HOW I wish you were here in Venice!" Albrecht wrote to Willibald. "There are so many nice companions among the Italians who seek my company more and more every day."

Dürer often sat up until after midnight writing to Willibald about his life in Venice. He was taking dancing lessons, he wrote, but after two lessons, he decided that he could not learn the steps.

"No one could get me to go there again!" he exclaimed.

He told Willibald about the altarpiece he was painting, and how Italian artists, jealous of his success, said that Dürer could not paint.

"Let me tell you," he wrote, "they are very unfriendly to me." Friends, fearing that Dürer might be poisoned, urged him not to eat meals with Venetian artists.

Dürer worked for six months on the altarpiece which showed the Madonna and Child surrounded by worshippers. The Pope, saints and priests were kneeling on the Virgin's right, while on her left knelt the German Emperor, Maximilian, and men and women from Germany who were living in Venice at that time. The Christ Child, leaning over His mother's arm, placed a wreath of roses on the Pope's head, while the Virgin placed another wreath on the head of the Emperor. Saint Dominic, standing beside the Virgin's throne, crowned a kneeling saint, and cherubs placed wreaths on the heads of the other worshippers. Dürer painted himself standing against a tree in the background, and on the scroll which he held, he lettered proudly:

"ALBRECHT DURER, THE GERMAN. 1506"

"There is no better image of the Virgin in the country," Dürer wrote about his altarpiece. Venice's most important citizens praised the glowing painting. The governors of the city called at his studio and offered him a salary if he would stay in Venice. But Albrecht knew that his family needed him in Nuremberg. He planned to return home soon, he wrote to Willibald.

"But," he added, "how I shall freeze after this sun!"

FEAST OF THE ROSE GARLANDS
  1506
    National Gallery, Prague

ONE BLUSTERY winter day in 1507, Albrecht arrived in Nuremberg. His mother was overjoyed to see her son again, and listened eagerly while he told her about the altarpiece he had painted in Italy. Agnes thought her husband looked very prosperous dressed in his Italian clothes. She was pleased when he told her that he had made money in Italy and that soon he planned to buy a new house.

In a few days Albrecht started to plan another altarpiece which had been commissioned by a German merchant, Jacob Heller. He chose as his subject the coronation of the Virgin. The top half of the picture would show the Virgin kneeling on a bank of clouds, while God the Father and Jesus placed a crown upon her head. Below stood a group of Christ's apostles, gazing in wonder at the vision above them.

Dürer spent weeks planning the picture. On blue paper he made drawings of each figure, and careful studies of the apostles' heads and feet and hands.

He wrote Heller that he had already spent so much time planning the picture that, unless the merchant sent him more money, he could not finish the work.

"It brings me no gain," he wrote, "and robs me of my work."

At last Heller agreed to send more money, and Dürer started to add coat after coat of brilliant color to the picture.

"And when it was finished," he wrote to Heller, "I painted it again twice. If it is kept clean, it will remain bright and fresh for five hundred years."

The painting did not last five hundred years. Two hundred years after it was finished, a fire broke out in the building where the picture was hanging, and before the flames could be put out, Dürer's great altarpiece had disappeared. But some of the most beautiful drawings in the world today are the studies which Dürer made for this famous painting.

HANDS OF AN APOSTLE
   Drawing for the Heller Altarpiece. 1508
   Albertina, Vienna

JUST INSIDE Nuremberg's city walls stood a tall house with a gabled roof. Its first two stories were made of stone and the four top stories were of plaster striped with timber. Into this big house Dürer moved with his family, one day in 1509. Agnes showed the servants where to place each piece of furniture, while Albrecht's asistants helped him arrange his workrooms on the two top floors.

Dürer was thirty-eight years old when he bought his fine new home. Not only was he Germany's best known artist, but he was also one of Nuremberg's important citizens. Scholars and writers who visited the city called at his home, and prosperous merchants asked him to paint pictures for their favorite churches.

As soon as he had finished the altarpiece for Jacob Heller, he started to plan another big altarpiece for the chapel of an old people's home in Nuremberg. The founder of the home, kindly old Matthaeus Landauer, who commissioned the work, also asked Dürer to design a frame for the painting.

Three years later, Dürer's finished painting was placed in its ornate frame and hung above the altar of the chapel.

Because the chapel was called The Holy Trinity and All Saints, Dürer showed the Trinity floating in clouds above a crowd of worshippers. At the top of the panel was the Dove, symbol of the Holy Ghost, and beneath was God the Father holding the crucified Christ. On either side knelt adoring saints. On a bank of clouds beneath the saints was a multitude of worshippers, many of whom were well known people of Dürer's day. Popes and Emperors, peasants and merchants, nuns and richly dressed ladies, all knelt before the heavenly vision. Long-haired, bearded Matthaeus Landauer knelt on the left beside a cardinal.

Dürer stood alone in the barren landscape beneath the worshippers. He held a tablet on which was printed in bold letters:

"MADE BY ALBRECHT DURER OF NUREMBERG IN THE YEAR 1511."

HE ADORATION OF THE TRINITY
The Landauer Altarpiece. 1511
Kunsthistorisches Museum, Vienna

As soon as Dürer's painting of the Holy Trinity was finished, Albrecht told his assistants to put away his paints and brushes, for he was ready at last to work on his engravings.

He loved to feel the sharp metal tool in his hands once more. Hour after hour he sat by the window in his workroom, digging out clean lines on a copper plate.

He made a set of fourteen small engravings which illustrated the last tragic hours of Christ's life. Each scene of Christ's Passion told a story in itself, so that the prints could be sold separately, and on each plate Dürer engraved the date and his well-known monogram. 𝔄

He filled the scenes with buildings, landscapes and figures dressed in the costumes of his day. He pictured the tragic moments of Jesus' Passion as if he had seen Christ's suffering himself. In many of the engravings the sorrowful face looks like the face of Dürer.

One moving picture showed Christ mocked by his enemies. Hands bound in front of Him, Jesus, wearing a crown of thorns, stood on a platform facing a cruel-looking man in a long cloak. Above the heads of the spectators in the background loomed three crosses which soldiers were carrying to a distant hill.

CHRIST MOCKED

From the Engraved Passion. 1512

Courtesy of the Metropolitan Museum of Art, New York

IN THE EVENINGS Dürer often sat in his oak-panelled study writing letters to his friends or making notes on his ideas about drawing and painting. He even tried writing poetry, although Willibald used to make fun of his friend's verses.

Dürer spent many hours reading the books of the scholar Erasmus who had admired Dürer's woodcuts. One book, *Handbook of the Christian Soldier,* impressed Dürer deeply. He pictured in his mind the Christian soldier whom Erasmus described, riding courageously along "the path of virtue," not fearing the dangers of the world around him.

Dürer designed a big engraving which showed a knight in armor riding along a rocky path. His eyes were fixed firmly on the goal ahead, so that he did not see the ghastly figure of death holding an hour-glass in front of him, or the leering horned devil behind him.

This big picture of the knight, death and the devil is one of Dürer's finest engravings, and so today it is called one of Dürer's "Master Engravings."

KNIGHT, DEATH AND DEVIL
Engraving. 1513
Courtesy of the Metropolitan Museum of Art, New York

DURER RAN print after print through his press, for art dealers in many countries of Europe were eager to buy Albrecht Dürer's engravings.

Albrecht's mother no longer sat in a booth at the Nuremberg fair, selling her son's prints, for she was far from well.

"She was more than once attacked by plague and other grave diseases," Dürer wrote about his mother. "She suffered much, but was never ill-tempered."

"Christ be with you," she used to say every time her favorite son came and went from the house.

One day Albrecht made a charcoal sketch of his mother's thin tired face. Her sad eyes and wrinkled brow told a tale of quiet suffering. Dürer wrote at the top of the picture, "This is the mother of Albrecht Dürer when she was 63 years old."

Two months later Albrecht's mother died.

"She looked far lovelier in death than she had in life," Dürer wrote, "and I buried her with all honor according to my means."

Albrecht felt strangely lonely without his mother to greet him as he came and went from his house. He often sat in his study thinking dark thoughts. Plunged in melancholy, he began to plan another big engraving.

DURER'S MOTHER
    Charcoal Drawing. 1514
    Kupferstichkabinett, Berlin

Dürer called his big engraving *Melancholia*. He had pondered deeply on the meaning of this word. Albrecht, himself, was often melancholy, because he felt he never could create a work of perfect beauty. He never gave up his search for perfect beauty. He started to write a book on how to draw the ideal figure and made diagrams showing the perfectly proportioned horse. But when he tried to find what perfect beauty was, he wrote, "What perfect beauty is—I know not."

In Dürer's big engraving, *Melancholia*, he showed a woman sitting on a step staring gloomily into space. This strange winged woman, untidily dressed, was supposed to represent the artist who realized he could not create the perfect work of art. The tools which she had used in vain were scattered all about her. A half-starved dog was lying at her feet and on a grindstone beside the idle woman sat a cupid scribbling on a pad. Unlike the artist who thought so deeply that he could not act, this child, too young to think, was working busily.

Each of the many objects in the picture had a special meaning, and the meanings of these symbols are hard to understand. But in this somber "master engraving" Dürer pictured the thoughts which were in his own mind.

MELANCHOLIA I

    Engraving. 1514

    Courtesy of the Metropolitan Museum of Art, New York

THE THOUGHTS which came to Dürer as he sat writing in his study were not always sad. The solitude of his room often brought him peace of mind. He imagined how the scholar Saint Jerome, who had lived one thousand years before, must have loved the seclusion of his cell.

In another big engraving Dürer pictured St. Jerome sitting at a table by the window working on his translation of the Bible. The sun streaming through the leaded panes lighted up the scholar's orderly study. The saint's pet lion, dozing at the entrance to the room, kept one eye slightly open in order to guard his master from intruders. A little dog, curled up beside the lion, was sleeping peacefully. Every object in the room was in its place. The saint's big hat, his hourglass, his manuscripts, scissors and rosary were hanging on the wall behind him. His slippers were neatly placed under the window seat, and standing on the corner of his table was a small crucifix. Nothing disturbed the meditation of the saint who had dedicated his work to God.

This peaceful picture of Saint Jerome is the third of Dürer's famous "Master Engravings."

SAINT JEROME IN HIS CELL
Engraving. 1514
Courtesy of the Metropolitan Museum of Art, New York

MAXIMILIAN I, Emperor of Germany, constantly called on the country's best artists and craftsmen to help him carry out his extravagant designs. Most of the work was left unfinished, for Maximilian never had enough money to pay the artists for their work. But the Emperor continued to make elaborate plans.

The art of bookmaking fascinated him. He collected old manuscripts and many printed books. He planned a new kind of printed prayer book. First he selected the prayers. He even rewrote some of them. Then he commissioned an artist to design a special type for the text which would look like hand-lettering. As soon as the bold black text was printed Maximilian asked Dürer to decorate the margins of each page.

Dürer picked out three different colored inks—red, violet and olive green — sharpened the point of his quill pen and started to work. His pen moved swiftly and evenly as he filled the borders with graceful leafy scrolls, human figures, different kinds of plans, and many curious objects. Birds and animals appear on every page, for Maximilian loved animals and kept one room in his palace filled with birds.

On one border Dürer illustrated the word "temptation." He drew a fox playing a flute in order to attract some hens which were on the other side of a stream.

In order to make the printed prayers look hand-lettered, Dürer drew red guide lines under each row of heavy black text.

Dürer made forty-five charming borders for the Emperor's prayer book, but before he could finish all the pages, Maximilian commissioned him to work on another ambitious scheme.

PAGE FROM THE PRAYER BOOK OF MAXIMILIAN I
1515
Staatsbibliothek, Munich
Photograph courtesy of the Metropolitan Museum of Art,
New York

MAXIMILIAN SPENT many hours with his secretary discussing plans for a series of woodcuts which would glorify his reign. He asked his court historian to outline the impressive program and appointed Albrecht Dürer designer-in-chief of the whole work.

For three years Dürer designed triumphal decorations for the Emperor, and Maximilian paid him a yearly pension for the work. He directed the designing of an enormous woodcut showing a triumphal arch which was decorated with columns, turrets, and ornaments of every kind. He asked Pirckheimer to choose subjects for many of the decorations. He made sketches of elaborate ornaments and of scenes from the Emperor's life to fill the panels between the columns. When the picture of the triumphal arch was finished, it was far too big to be printed from one block. The enormous print, which was almost twelve feet high, was made from one-hundred and ninety-two wood blocks. It is the biggest woodcut that has ever been made.

As soon as Dürer had finished working on the triumphal arch, he started to carry out the Emperor's plan for a magnificent procession. He drew trumpeters and pipers, hunters and soldiers, and riders carrying banners. He made drawings of chariots and one of an ornate triumphal car in which the Emperor rode in state, accompanied by goddesses representing different virtues. Even the wheels and the reins of the chariot were carefully labelled with names which glorified the Emperor's reign.

Maximilian did not live to see the printed woodcut of the procession, and some of his plans were never put on paper. But when the prints of the long parade were placed end to end the picture measured almost sixty yards.

SMALL TRIUMPHAL CAR
Woodcut. 1518/19
Courtesy of the Metropolitan Museum of Art, New York

GAY BANNERS were hanging from the windows of every house in Augsburg one June day in 1518 and flags were flying from the Emperor's castle high above the town, for on this day delegates from every part of Germany were meeting with the Emperor to discuss affairs of state. From Nuremberg came the famous artist Albrecht Dürer, who had been chosen by that city to represent his town. Maximilian received the delegates in his palace and here, for the first time, Dürer met the Emperor for whom he had been working for so many years. Maximilian welcomed the artist cordially and, after the meeting was over, agreed to sit while Dürer drew his portrait.

In the Emperor's little study overlooking the city, Dürer made a charcoal drawing of Maximilian. He worked quickly, stopping once in a while so that the Emperor could criticize the sketch. Sometimes Maximilian tried to show Dürer what he wanted him to draw, but the charcoal would crumble under his heavy grasp. When he asked the artist to tell him the secret of his skill, Dürer replied that drawing was his job; the Emperor, he said, had more important work to do.

Dürer had often pictured Maximilian's face in his drawings for the triumphal decorations, but the portraits were copies of other artists' pictures. So when he had finished his charcoal drawing of the Emperor, he wrote in the corner of the picture, "Here is the Emperor Maximilian, as I, Albrecht Dürer, have pictured him, high up in his tiny little cabinet in Augsburg in the year 1518."

Soon after his return to Nuremberg, Dürer made a woodcut from his drawing, but the Emperor never saw the finished print. Only a few months after Dürer had made his charcoal sketch, Maximilian, Albrecht's loyal friend and patron, died.

PORTRAIT OF MAXIMILIAN I
  Charcoal Drawing. 1518
  Albertina, Vienna

THE NEW Emperor of Germany, Charles V, was not interested in finishing Maximilian's elaborate plans, and Dürer worried that his yearly pension would be cut off. So in the summer of 1520, he decided to meet the Emperor in Flanders where Charles was being crowned. He told Agnes to pack her best clothes for he was taking her with him to Antwerp. Then he filled a chest with tall slim sketchbooks, pens and silver point pencils, and with copies of his woodcuts and engravings which he planned to sell.

One day in August, Albrecht, Agnes and her maid arrived in Antwerp. Artists, craftsmen and scholars welcomed the famous German artist. They helped him find comfortable rooms and they showed him the sights of the city. The enormous cathedral impressed Dürer greatly, and he marveled at the mayor's new house, "The like of which I have never seen in German lands," he wrote in his diary.

The markets, filled with curious objects from distant lands, fascinated Dürer. He bought buffalo horns, dried fishes, shells and pieces of coral. He was delighted when a friend gave him a wooden rosary and a hundred oysters for one of his prints. He kept a careful account of his expenses and of the profits from his sales of woodcuts and engravings.

The painters of Antwerp gave a banquet in Dürer's honor.

"As I was led to the table," he wrote, "the crowd stood on both sides as though a great Lord were ushered in . . . and late at night they saw me home in state with torchlights."

Dürer filled sketchbooks with drawings of buildings and bits of landscapes. He drew the fishing boats in the Antwerp harbor and the houses with tall pointed roofs.

In the fall Dürer set off for Aix-la-Chapelle, the town where Charles was being crowned.

"There I saw all manner of lordly splendor," he wrote. When the ceremony was over he followed the Emperor to Cologne, and there, "after much labor and exertion," Dürer wrote, he persuaded Charles to promise him a pension.

ANTWERP HARBOR
   Pen Drawing. 1520
   Albertina, Vienna

WHEN DURER returned to Antwerp, one November day, friends told him that an enormous fish had been washed up on the shore of the island of Zeeland. Dürer, eager to see this curious sight, put his sketchbooks in a bag and set off in search of a whale.

The tide had washed the "great fish" out to sea before Dürer arrived in Zeeland. Hoping to find the fish on a nearby island, he boarded a ship with a group of disappointed passengers. All that day the little boat tossed on a choppy sea, while the passengers looked in vain for the whale.

A fierce wind was blowing when the captain tried to land his ship on the shore that evening. Dürer, standing in the prow, watched the sailors desperately trying to pull the boat up onto the beach. Suddenly the captain shouted that the mooring rope had broken and that the ship, without its crew, was moving out to sea.

"So I spoke to the captain," Albrecht wrote later, "that he should take courage and have hope in God, and that he should consider what was to be done." Calmed by Dürer's words, the captain showed the passengers how to put up a sail and soon the boat was landed on the shore. Early the next morning, Dürer boarded the ship again, but he never saw the whale, for, he wrote, "The tide had carried her off again."

Dürer returned to Antwerp exhausted by his trip. "In the third week after Easter a violent fever seized me," he wrote in his diary. But as soon as the fever left him, he decided to take another trip, for he was anxious to see the cities of Bruges and Ghent before he returned to Germany.

In Bruges he admired the paintings of the great Flemish artists, and in Ghent, "I was deemed a great man at once," he wrote. He was taken up into the tower of the cathedral, "And there I beheld the great wondrous city," he continued. "Next I saw the lions and drew one in silver point." He also made a sketch of a walrus which had been caught off the coast of Flanders.

LION IN TWO POSITIONS
Silver Point Drawing. 1521
Kupferstichkabinett, Berlin

HEAD OF WALRUS
Pen Drawing. 1521
British Museum, London

Soon after his return to Antwerp, Albrecht started to buy presents to take to his friends in Nuremberg, and to say goodby to the friends who had welcomed him so cordially. The governors of the city offered Dürer a house and salary if he would stay in Antwerp, but Albrecht refused because he wanted to see his home again.

Then one day as Albrecht was packing his treasures, the King of Denmark arrived in Antwerp and commissioned Dürer to paint his portrait.

In a few hours Dürer made a portrait drawing of the King. "He was a manly handsome man," Albrecht wrote. So pleased was King Christian with the picture, that he invited the artist to dinner and offered to pay him well if he would make a painting from his drawing.

The next day the King set off for Brussels to meet the German Emperor, and with him went Albrecht, Agnes and her maid. When they arrived at the city gates the German Emperor and a brilliant train of courtiers rode out to greet the visiting King. In the evening Charles gave a splendid banquet in honor of King Christian and invited Dürer to watch the regal feast. When, a few days later, King Christian entertained the Emperor, he asked Dürer to sit at the table with the royal guests.

Albrecht was entranced with the gifts which the Emperor presented to the King. In his diary he described these treasures which had been brought back from newly discovered Mexico.

"Strange garments, bedspreads and all sorts of wondrous things," he wrote.

As soon as the portrait of the King was finished, Albrecht, his wife and maid said good-by to Flanders. Three days later they arrived in Cologne, where they boarded a boat which took them up the Rhine toward Nuremberg. Dürer took out his sketchbook and started to draw. He sketched a young girl wearing a fancy cap, and on the same page, he made a drawing of his stern, unsmiling wife, her hard face framed by a scarf which was wrapped about her neck.

PORTRAIT OF DURER'S WIFE AND GIRL
IN COLOGNE HEADDRESS
    Silver Point Drawing. 1521
    Albertina, Vienna

DURER balanced his account book as soon as he returned to Nuremberg.

"I have come out with a deficit," he wrote in his diary. But he did not regret his year in Flanders, for he had brought back sketchbooks filled with drawings. In Antwerp he had bought a cage full of little monkeys to add to his collection. It amused him to see the lively beasts scampering and capering like dancing men. One day he drew a sketch of little monkeys swinging into a dance.

Although Dürer was only fifty years old, he was thin and haggard, for the fever which had attacked him in Flanders had left him weak. He spent more and more time in his home working on small engravings and writing the books he had started before he went to Flanders.

In clear simple language he explained problems in geometry, which would be helpful to artists, architects and engineers. He illustrated the books with diagrams. He showed how to construct different kinds of letters, and gave instructions about designing triumphal monuments. He outlined a plan for a model city, and wrote a chapter on how to fortify a town.

"It is better that a ruler should spend much money and remain," he wrote, "than that . . . he should be overrun by his enemy." When the book was finished he dedicated it to Pirckheimer.

He wrote a history of the Dürer family. He told about his hard-working father, his pious mother and about his own childhood. Remembering the rough treatment he had received when he was a student in Wolgemut's studio, he decided to write a booklet on teaching art to children. "If the child worketh too hard, so that he fall under the hand of melancholy," he wrote, "that he be enticed therefrom by merry music."

Dürer continued with his studies of what made a perfect work of art. "The more one approaches nature, the more artistic thy work becomes," he wrote. But, he believed that the artist must always create something new.

"If it is possible for him to live forever," Dürer wrote, "he would always have to pour forth something new."

MONKEYS DANCING
Pen Drawing. 1523
Kuntsmuseum, Basel

"**N**OW THAT I have just painted two panels upon which I have bestowed more trouble than on any other paintings," Dürer wrote to the governors of Nuremberg in 1526. "I considered none more worthy to keep them . . . than your honors . . . because of the particular love and affection which I bear to . . . this honorable town."

For one year Dürer had been working on the paintings which he had decided to present to the city of Nuremberg. Into two tall narrow panels he fitted the more than life-size figures of Christ's apostles. Saint John, in a red cloak, stood on the left, his head lowered as if absorbed in the book he was reading. Behind him stood Saint Peter, holding a key, his bald head bent in prayer. On the right stood two fierce defenders of the faith. Saint Paul, robed in white, held a Bible and a sword. His expression was watchful and austere. Fiery Saint Mark, eyes blazing, stood in the background.

The governors of Nuremberg proudly hung Dürer's panels in the town hall. A few days later Albrecht and Agnes received a generous gift of money from the city fathers. The panels of the four apostles were Dürer's last big paintings.

The fever which Dürer had caught in Flanders attacked him more and more often. He was only fifty-five years old, but "he was withered like a bundle of straw," Willibald wrote to a friend.

Even during his illness he continued to work on his book on proportions, striving constantly to find what made perfect beauty, and never giving up his search for truth.

"All things pass away with time," Dürer once wrote. "Truth, alone, endures forever."

Then suddenly, one spring day in 1528, Albrecht Dürer died. He left behind him almost one hundred paintings, over a thousand drawings and hundreds of beautiful woodcuts and engravings.

"I hold my art at a very mean value," Dürer wrote before he died. "Let every man strive to better these my errors according to his powers. Would to God it were possible for me to see the work of the mighty masters to come!"

THE FOUR APOSTLES
1526
Alte Pinakothek, Munich

BIBLIOGRAPHY

Cust, Lionell. *The Paintings and Drawings of Albrecht Dürer*. Seeley and Co. Ltd., London. The Macmillan Company, New York, 1897

DuColombier, Pierre. *Albrecht Dürer*. Albin Michel Editeur, Paris, 1927

Durant, Will. *The Reformation, A History of European Civilization from Wyclif to Calvin. 1300-1564*. Simon and Schuster, New York, 1957

Dürer, Albrecht. *Journal de Voyage dans le Pays Bas*. Traduit et commente par J. A. Goris. Editions de la connaissance, S. A. Bruxelles, 1937

Designs of the Prayer Book, Introduction by J. B. Bernhart. R. Ackermann's Lithographic Press, 1817

Fenyo, Iván. *Albrecht Dürer,* Translated from the Hungarian by Ann Biener Tauber. Coruina, Budapest, 1956

Headlam, Cecil. *The Story of Nuremberg,* with illustrations by Miss H. M. James and with woodcuts. J. M. Dent and Sons Ltd., London, 1911

Knackfuss, H. *Dürer,* Translated by Campbell Dodgson, Bielefeld and Leipzig, Velhagen and Keasing, 1900

LaFarge, John. *Great Masters*. McClure, Phillips and Co. New York, 1903

Moore, T. Sturge. *Albrecht Dürer*. A. D. Duckworth and Co., London, Charles Scribners Sons, New York, 1905

Neumeyer, Alfred. *Dürer* (Traduction Française de S. Loussert). Les Editions G. Crès et Cie. Paris, 1929

Panofsky, Erwin. *The Life and Art of Albrecht Dürer*. Princeton University Press, Princeton, 1955

Thausing, Moriz. *The Life of Albrecht Dürer,* Translated from the German. John Murray, Albe Marle Street. London, 1882

Terrasse, Charles. *Dürer, Biographie de l'artiste. Analyse des oeuvres reproduites*. Librairie Renouard, Henri Laurens, Editeur. Paris, 1935

Waetzoldt, Wilhelm. *Dürer and His Times*. Phaidon Publishers Inc., Distributed by Oxford University Press. New York, 1950

Watercolors by Albrecht Dürer. Thirty-two plates in color selected and with an introduction by Anna Maria Otto. The Macmillan Co. New York. Holbein-Verlag. Basel, 1954

INDEX